12 Hours of Madness

C.J. Sahadeo

ISBN: 978-976-96561-0-9

A GENTLE WARNING

The poems contained in this chapbook sometimes deals with difficult and intense subject matter. Persons with known triggers are asked to exercise caution when reading.

CONTENTS

ACKNOWLEDGMENTS

God and my family made this possible.

Tap, tap.

Tap, tap.

Tick-tock.

Tick-tock.

Lub-dub.

Lub-dub.

Beep, beep.

Beep, beep.

Sound and silence, intertwined, inextricable from the other, opposites, causes, tangled like nerves into flesh and thread into fabric and the beat of the heart to the throbbing of arteries.

Madness and sanity. What are they but mirrors that kiss? Golden streams that lead to black waterfalls and silver lakes.

Like sound and silence, they are tied together, knotted in the cerebral cortex, married in the flesh of the brain, divorced in the holding of morals, commit secret trysts in situations so dark, so demanding that lines blur and minds break.

Light and dark, they say, sane and insane.

But sometimes madness is the gentle edge of sanity; softening the impossible, giving hope to hunches and life to dreams.

Sanity, the harsh line of reality, cutting where madness dares to dream, to hold on, to fight.

So maybe sometimes, we all need a little madness in our lives. Because what may have been thought to be madness, may turn out to be the sanest thing in our lives.

I AM AFRAID

No, No,

Write me this story,

I want to know how it goes,

I'm about to live it,

So tell me,

Tell me how it goes,

Tell me the traps,

The tricks,

The trials,

Tell me this tale,

I am lost

and I will be broken,

I do not know how to take

my grounded bones and use

them as mortar for my

hard earned, bloody blocks.

I AM AFRAID

Tell me the journey,

Give me the map,

I am afraid,

Give me hope,

Give me courage,

Tell me I see an end

beyond the peace of death.

Give me soothing rain,

Tell me the thunder will hear

when I cry,

Will send the lightening,

Tell me the storm

will cradle me in its winds,

That the clouds will roll back to

show me the stars,

Tell me the mountains will call me friend

and I would call them home.

Give me bonfires in the dead of night,

Give me warm words,

Warm understanding,

Care,

Give me songs on the wind,

Moisture on the air,

Warm sunlight,

And lighting bugs.

Tell me this tale

Tell me this story,

Tell me,

Tell me there is some way that it is worth it,

Tell me that I'll find it worth it,

Tell me,

For I am afraid.

THE STREETS

360 edges

and a bag full of real,

I am here to steal the deal,

Gonna work until I keel

over,

There's pot in my pocket,

that I won't smoke,

Hard liquor in my bag,

that I won't drink,

'cept thru my skin,

peeled open

and bleeding.

I don't dull my raw edges,

I feel them grind every day,

Sharpen my broken mind,

Use it to cut my way up,

I am run down,

Homeless,

Son of a gun,

But I aim higher,

I aim true,

Ain't no scum streets

for me every day,

No gang bangers

whispering threats in my ear,

No knife tickling my ribs

and sweating fear,

Imma done with sitting in these

broken streets,

I've got plans,

And a ruthless heart in me,

The whole city grid may come for me,

But I'll scream back at the streets,

"You never owned me!"

LOVE IN BLUE AND BLACK

Forceful entry,

It's all door edges

and bruises,

'I-love-you's' in blue and black,

Dressed over with soft red petals

and *"Shh, shh,*

It's okay,

Don't you know it's

gotta be this way?

Silly, silly spouse,

Don't I tell you what to do?

Look you didn't listen

and you got burned,"

Generous care

in melting lips,

gorgeous food,

Have me drunk

on you're-too-good-to-be-trues,

And my bones keep cracking,

Sending out spikes of warnings,

entreaties to leave

before it's too late,

Shivers of disgust when fingers trail skin,

I say its pleasure,

Lie to let it all in,

Survive,

But its way past the date

of expiration,

I should be gone,

My lover's hands have my name

on them

as sure as bullets

call out to their targets,

And I'm a tragedy in the waking,

A crime in the making,

But how do I let go?

Get free?

Get past this traitorous part of me

that whispers I love them

and they love me?

CREATIVE

It's all in my head,

These bursts of colour,

Triggered by song and sound and sight,

A torrent of words

tingling my fingertips,

Sparking along my nerves

like live wires

and wild fires

and storms of emotion,

They call this creative bent,

I call it life,

Can't be any other way,

Can't go any day

without words and images

soaring through my head.

It's jarring this bent of ours,

People say it's a process,

But that word always

conjures up a feeling of order,

But I'm here,

Pushing the ragged edges

of phrases together

in the hopes

of finding poetry

and building worlds

with stories of their own.

I struggle,

And I cry,

I am frustrated for hours,

I spend hours lost,

Pouring out words,

Tapping keys,

Sketching maps,

Crafting psyches,

Building rapport,

And at the end of the day,

it's a good tired.

ADDICTION

I chase the high,

Half-high on the chase,

Half-mad that I am being

made to run,

I want control,

I lose it

to gain it,

I don't gain it,

But still I'm trying.

Alcohol?

I'm sipping amber,

Feeling the burn of hard topazes

cutting down my throat,

Slicing the ropes of my inhibitions.

Drugs?

I'm in that cloud nine,

That superhuman,

That dream,

While I inject myself straight

into the ninth circle outside,

Awake but not alive.

Sex is hell,

Pure delightful sin

and everything I hate,

But I'm an addict,

And there's nothing

I don't do to self-destruct,

Even put up with hands I hate.

Every dare is a vice,

I'm stone cold sober,

And raving mad

If there's anything good for me,

it's bad for me,

Preserving me

isn't the goal

I want this bubble-head dead,

This airy girl

with nothing inside but spaces to fill.

IMPENDING EXTINCTION

There's a hollowness in

my legs

as my muscles shrivel,

an ominous cracking

of these proud bones

heralds their

decent to powder.

Bitter grapes

are these old eyes,

And the sides of this

tongue are whetted sharp

by the years.

Wisdom gained by folly,

Jolly youth and stupid

waste of time,

I am of a mind

to march forward,

And plant armies,

Seed dominion,

Lead overtaking,

Save lives

from the hands of the

wildly inexperienced,

The poor fool

I once was.

There is work to be done,

A necessary carnage

for the cure,

A healing,

An atoning,

A vision to set free,

to realize.

I have lived long enough

to gain knowledge,

to see the start

of the solution,

But my hands tremble

And my fingers won't bend

My breath cuts short,

Halving the time for my plans.

Yet still I soldier on,

There is still much

I can do,

Must do,

I do not care

that this aged

frame is failing,

I do not accept it,

The world may think

it natural,

That the future is

for the young,

And the old must fade,

But I?

I rage against extinction.

WAR

They don't ask,

These leaders of ours,

These military commanders

who march our future into havoc,

And cause our future to lie bleeding

on the streets of once-home,

Crying futilely for parents

that will never hear,

And never rise.

They don't ask,

They start wars,

and hide in bunkers,

And order their people

to their death,

While civilians flutter among the ruins

of the past,

seeking shelter

in twisted skeletons,

And beg the charity of strangers

from half-way around the world.

There are so many dead eyes

among the living,

Old eyes

in the young,

Despair and determination

in soldiers and civilians

both,

And nobody is innocent

when the bloody rain stops

and the scorching earth cools,

No one who still survives.

You don't know war until you're sitting covered in a stranger's blood,

weeping as if they had been family.

Because you are,

were,

blood relation to them now.

The same terror and trauma

thrummed through your veins,

etched into your bones.

You screamed together,

ran together,

cried together,

raged together

and died together,

splattered in each other's blood,

tangled in your intestines,

intimate in the tissues of crushed limbs

and rhythmless hearts.

This is war.

It's a tyrant that only pretends

to care about winners

but everyone is a loser

under its iron fist.

Winners are only those

who don't lose something,

And everyone loses something in war,

Some of us just lose more.

HOME

I dream,

I dream dreams

that will never be mine,

And yet, yet,

I work for them,

Hold them close to my heart

Guard them jealously,

Like they are gold,

And more precious than

gold could ever dream to be

I dream,

And I ache,

This thing I want

may never be mine,

I may not be able to handle

the scope of it,

But oh, how I mean

to suffer for it,

To try and try,

To grit teeth,

And grind knuckles,

To hold temper,

And tongue,

And dispense

soft touches

and gentle words,

And entangle encouragement

with punishment.

I dream,

Safe spaces

for broken spirits,

And wounded hearts,

And fractured minds,

Tiny feet,

And teenaged ones,

The lost and left behind,

The confused and the jaded,

The too old in too young bodies.

I dream

of havens

in simple walls,

Protected places

where laughter can

grow once more,

And tears don't carry

a price,

I dream of harbors

for shattered ships

and sabotaged souls.

I dream of home.

FORMULATED EXPRESSION

A sweeping arc 0 to 60,

A leg and then an arm,

360 turn,

180 measured between legs

while arms are twisting

in the air,

Flowing through angles

gracefully,

Never committing to one

before the other is sliding up,

Always changing,

Metamorphosis measured

by the beat of

the music.

Swirls on xyz planes,

Mirror image

on silvered walls,

Body aloft

in a tangle

of formulas,

Plotting points in space,

Choreographed by algorithms.

My form

is numbers in motion,

Each jump is a cascade

of computation,

I wrap matrices through

my bones,

Sew transposition into

my muscles

Subtract each exhale,

Inhalation is addition.

My repetitions are

squares and cubes,

The root of me lies here

in the dance floor,

Drawn to the apex

Of my axes,

The zero of stillness,

Before I burst

into breathless

motion.

FEVER

I am sinking into a haze

of heat and pain,

Cracking thirst

snaps at the back of my throat,

Dry hurt

echoing dully

through my lungs.

I am simmering

in the aching warmth

of fever dreams,

Where you smile

at me,

eyes bright and sparkling,

Joy so rich and fresh

I could drink it,

Quench the yawning

pit of loneliness.

I toss and turn,

Buried in blankets,

Unable to release

myself from

The fever-fueled

visions

where you are here,

Here and not there,

Not under cool, earth

and flowers misting

in the gentle rain.

Glazed eyes,

Parched lips,

They say I should strive

to be cured,

Process the fact,

Go through the process

that leaves you an aching scar

instead of a bleeding wound,

I defy them all,

My fever-bright eyes

see you,

Maybe this is sick,

But I miss you.

So I'll lie here,

Tangled up

in fever dreams,

Until the heat of you

consumes me,

Rather than face the

cold of your corpse.

GLASS

Glass walls,

Glass houses,

Glass heart,

Glass shards of a shattered

throat.

I've been screaming

words too strong

for it to contain,

Screaming too loud to be heard.

I'm fractured bones,

A fragile spine

cracking under the weight

of a heavy head,

a heart that tips

the scales,

Sends the feather fluttering

to the ground.

I am guilty of

so much,

I throw stones,

I live encased

in clear, brittle walls,

I scream,

I don't sew myself

together,

I rage,

Throw shattered pieces

of myself

at others,

Hurt,

Hurt,

Because I'm hurt,

And screaming

until spider cracks

shadow my lungs

does nothing,

But it's all I can seem to do.

I am a statuette

breaking on the waves

of life,

I am a hazard,

Splinter fingers,

And jagged teeth,

Sharp tongue,

Skin in

layers and layers

of ragged peaks

and valleys.

Glass human,

In a glass cage,

Shattering,

Day by day,

Piece by piece,

Screaming until they break,

To be seen,

But perhaps,

Silence,

Silence might be heard.

Silence or sound,

Silence or screaming until

they shatter,

Fly apart

in a glass storm,

to shriek

messages in blood

and shards

of human will.

ALIVE

I am sinking,

And sailing,

I rise and fall,

I scream and roar,

I am pain

and determination,

Pleasure and fear.

I am this,

This fighting,

This moving,

This breathing,

And bleeding,

And healing,

And craving,

And hating,

And loving so deeply

the love scars me

and tattoos my bones

in spinning patterns

of dizzy minds,

and fluttering stomachs.

I am this,

This heaving breath

of exertion,

These tears of joy,

and hurt,

These running legs,

And pumping arms,

These echoes in my mind

that urge me to

never give up,

To keep going,

To keep pushing,

To stop and breath,

To drink in

this nectar

of sweet, sweet life,

the sheer ecstasy

of warmth and care,

To live in the liquid sunlight,

To dance in the firefly

moonlight,

To laugh

real and long,

Let the echoes of mirth

roll on for eons and eons.

I am this,

This pulse,

This heartbeat,

This lifeline,

This signal through space,

This call that says

I am here,

I am alive,

I am real,

I exist

in the planes of

of life,

Between the pages of time

and march of history,

I walk and I change

I affect,

Each throb of blood

carries me closer to my goals,

Each peak and valley

denotes the sum of my life.

I am this,

This pulsing star,

This rising sun,

This breathing earth,

This beating heart,

This bleeding mind.

I am this,

Alive.

ABOUT THE AUTHOR

Christianna loves the ocean, music, and sleeping. She has been writing since the age of eleven and since then has graduated from carrying around a pocket full of papers half-scribbled on to carrying around a smartphone filled with story notes and stories. She completed her Bachelors of Science degree in Medical Laboratory Technology at the College of Science, Technology and Applied Arts of Trinidad and Tobago and now spends more time culturing bacteria than the average person. Christianna lives in the beautiful twin island state of Trinidad and Tobago with her family and her child (read: pet dog). When she's not reading, she's writing. When she's not writing, she's probably feeding her coffee addiction or doodling with pretty much anything she can get her hands on.